HOT TOPICS

PLASTIC POLLUTION

D0001856

Geof Knight

YA

Heinemann
LIBRARY

Chicago, Illinois

www.capstonepub.com
Visit our website to find out
more information about
Heinemann-Raintree books.

To order:
☎ Phone 888-454-2279
🖥 Visit www.capstonepub.com
    to browse our catalog and order online.

© 2012 Heinemann Library
an imprint of Capstone Global Library, LLC
Chicago, Illinois

Visit our website at www.heinemannraintree.com

Edited by Adam Miller, Nick Hunter and
  Diyan Leake
Designed by Philippa Jenkins
Original illustrations © Capstone Global
  Library Ltd 2012
Picture research by Mica Brancic
Production by Eirian Griffiths and Alison Parsons
Originated by Capstone Global Library Ltd
Printed and bound in the USA by Corporate
Graphics

15 14 13 12 11
10 9 8 7 6 5 4 3 2 1

**Library of Congress Cataloging-in-Publication
Data**
Knight, Geof (Geoffrey David)
  Plastic pollution / Geof Knight.
    p. cm.—(Hot topics)
  Includes bibliographical references and index.
  ISBN 978-1-4329-6039-1 (hb)—ISBN 978-1-
4329-6047-6 (pb) 1. Plastics—Environmental
aspects—Juvenile literature. I. Title.
  TP1125.K55 2012
  363.72'88—dc23   2011017911

Acknowledgments
The author and publisher are grateful to the
following for permission to reproduce copyright
material: Alamy pp. 13 (© Ambient Images
Inc.), 16 (© Mark Boulton); Corbis pp. 8 (In
Pictures/© Stuart Freedman), 25 (epa/© Jane
Hahn), 26 (epa/ © Jane Hahn), 29 (Reuters/©
Regis Duvignau), 31 (epa/© Melyn R. Acosta),
37 (Reuters/© Jean-Paul Pelissier), 45 (© Roger
Ressmeyer), 53 (epa/© Armando Babani);
FWC Photo p. 20 (Cathy Connolly); Getty
Images pp. 11 (Bloomberg/Jonathan Alcorn),
15 (Bloomberg/Tara Zorovich), 32 (AFP/Hector
Mata); Photoshot pp. 38 (© Woodfall), 51
(© UPPA); Shutterstock pp. 4 (© Alterfalter), 7
(© Christian Darkin), 18 (© Holbox), 23 (© Joe
Gough), 34 (© Kotomiti), 40 (© Beror), 43
(© Morgan Lane Photography), 48 (© fthes).

Cover photograph of a sea turtle (*Chelonia
mydas*) mistaking a plastic cup for jellyfish in
the Pacific Ocean, reproduced with permission
of Photolibrary (Oxford Scientific (OSF)/Paulo de
Oliveira).

Every effort has been made to contact copyright
holders of material reproduced in this book.
Any omissions will be rectified in subsequent
printings if notice is given to the publishers.

Disclaimer
All the internet addresses (URLs) given in this
book were valid at the time of going to press.
However, due to the dynamic nature of the
internet, some addresses may have changed, or
sites may have changed or ceased to exist since
publication. While the author and publishers
regret any inconvenience this may cause readers,
no responsibility for any such changes can be
accepted by either the author or the publishers.

CONTENTS

Some words are printed in bold, **like this**. You can find out what they mean by looking in the glossary.

A WORLD OF PLASTIC POLLUTION

■ Plastic is overwhelming the world.

How many plastic products do you use in your everyday life? Plastic is everywhere—from the tube your toothpaste comes in to the chair you sit on at school. It is an important part of electronic items such as toys, computers, and cell phones. Sometimes, plastic is an unseen part of our environment. For example, it is used for pipes in houses, essential parts in cars, and even in airplanes and rockets. It is resistant to harmful substances, good for insulation, and exceptionally versatile.

Plastic is a manufactured material, made by humans. It is flexible and lightweight but also very strong. Plastic is more able to stand wear than other materials, such as wood, metal, or paper. However, although plastic is a long-lasting material, it is often used in disposable (throwaway) products such as drink bottles, grocery bags, utensils, pens, and diapers.

WHY PEOPLE USE PLASTIC

- Plastic is very strong, and chemicals do not wear it away quickly. It provides nonbreakable packages for dangerous liquids. Liquid leaning products are also packaged in plastic for safety.

- Plastic insulates (protects) against heat and electricity. Electrical appliances, leads, outlets, and wiring are usually made or covered with plastic. Plastic pot and pan handles protect against burning heat. Plastic is also used in the foam core of fridges and freezers, in insulated cups, coolers, and microwave cookware.

- Plastic is very light. Compared to stone, concrete, steel, copper, or aluminum, all plastics are lightweight.

- Plastic is versatile. It can be processed into very thin fibers or molded into large car parts such as dashboards and bumpers. It can be foamed into **polystyrene** or mixed with liquids to become adhesives or paints.

- Plastic comes in a countless range of types and colors. It can be made to mimic fabrics such as cotton, silk, and wool fibers; feel like stone such as porcelain and marble; or look like metals such as aluminum and zinc. Plastics also come as clear sheets and flexible film.

Fantastic plastic

Plastic has become an important and useful part of our world. But the strength and durability of plastic has a flip side. The world now finds itself polluted with disposable plastics that will not go away. They do not decompose, or break down, as fast as wood or paper. And when they do start to break down, they are harmful to the environment.

For these reasons and others, plastics are convenient and helpful. But, as this book will examine, plastic has become controversial. Plastic increasingly threatens the environment as pollution on land and in the ocean.

Problems with plastic

Plastic is amazing. Without it, life would be less convenient. But the convenience of plastic has come at a price, mostly because so many plastics are used for disposable items that people throw away. The problem is that the items do not ever go "away" from the planet; they pollute it.

A recent realization

By the 1980s, there was so much visible plastic pollution that it was impossible to ignore. Plastic bottles littered beaches, plastic bags fluttered from tree branches, and disposable diapers polluted canals and rivers. Plastic was piling up so high because it does not **biodegrade**, or break down into the environment, very easily. People were throwing more and more disposable products away. This meant that **landfill** sites were filling up with items that may take up to a thousand years to decompose. All of those trillions of plastic bags, styrofoam cups, bottles, and plastic utensils will remain in landfills for a very long time. Suddenly, "disposable" did not seem so convenient any more.

Another cause for concern was the effect plastic pollution was having on wildlife. On land and in the ocean, plastic threatens to poison animals. In turn, this affects our food supply.

This book will examine these problems of plastic pollution and many others. But it will also examine ways that plastic pollution might be fought, through people educating themselves about the problem and, then, taking action. Due to the amount of plastic pollution already taking place, people need to think about what to do with it. They also need to think about how to stop adding to the problem.

How plastic is made

Plastic comes from **petroleum** (oil). Scientists **refine** oil through a heating process. This produces ethylene and propylene, which are the chemical building blocks of plastic. These chemicals are then combined with other chemicals to form a **polymer**. A polymer is a chain of a chemical unit such as **carbon**, hydrogen, oxygen, or silicon. Plastics are basically very long chains of these chemical units, sticking together to make the material for items we know. However, not all polymers are plastic. Tar, shellac, tortoiseshell, and horn, for example, are natural polymers.

Many plastics come from oil.

Next, plastic polymers are mixed with additional chemicals. Then, this mixture is heated and molded to create plastic in a "raw" form, such as plastic pellets, powder, flakes, or paste. This raw plastic is sold to manufacturers that heat the raw plastic again to mold it into different shapes to make their products. Materials called plasticizers are added to the mixture to increase flexibility and toughness. Fillers are added to improve particular features such as hardness or resistance to shock. Colors are also added.

Plastics are divided into two classes, based on whether or not they can be formed again after being melted. **Thermoplastics** can be melted and formed again and again. **Thermosets** are plastics which, once formed, are destroyed by heating. (They will not form again after melting.)

The history of plastic

Throughout history, materials such as tortoiseshell and ivory have been highly valued for their beauty, toughness, and flexibility. Ivory was used to make things such as piano keys, while tortoiseshell was often used to make combs and small bowls. Since ivory comes from elephant tusks, and tortoiseshell comes from the shells of turtles, they are difficult materials to get and very expensive. From around the mid-1800s, scientists were trying to develop substances that had the same look, feel, and toughness as ivory and tortoiseshell, but which could be made quickly and cheaply. Success came in 1862. An English inventor named Alexander Parkes introduced Parkesine. Although Parkesine is considered to be the first plastic, it was actually made partly from cellulose from plant walls. It would not be until 1907 that the first truly synthetic (human-made) plastic was developed.

■ Kevlar is one of the strongest plastics in the world. It is used in bulletproof vests and other body armor.

SPOTLIGHT ON BAKELITE

When Bakelite products appeared in the 1920s and 1930s (see the timeline opposite), they did not mimic ivory or tortoiseshell. Bakelite looked and felt different from anything seen before. Advertising was a growing industry at the time, and its power helped Bakelite's appeal. Bakelite was modern and new, not made from the same materials as old-fashioned items. After World War II, Bakelite itself was replaced by plastics that were quicker and cheaper to manufacture.

Key dates in the development of plastic

1907	*Bakelite* was the first completely synthetic plastic. It was made from coal tar, rapidly hardened, and was easily moldable. Unlike earlier plastics which melted easily, Bakelite kept its shape even under stress and heat. It is no longer made today, but, in its time, it was used for jewelry, telephones, clocks, and radios.
1920	*Polyvinyl chloride (PVC)* is a great insulator and protector because of its hardness. Today, about 75 percent of PVC materials are used for piping, tubing, flooring, roofing, and electrical cable insulation.
1933	*Cling wrap* was sprayed on fighter planes to protect against rust! In 1953, the chemical company Dow noticed that it clung to, and sealed, almost any surface. They began selling it as rolls of cling wrap that we use today for wrapping food to keep it fresh.
1933	*Polyethylene (PET)* was first used to insulate radar systems in planes. Today, **PET** is used in milk cartons, drink bottles, plastic bags, and food storage containers. It is currently the most widely used plastic.
1938	*Teflon* was originally used to coat machinary's metal parts in factories. It is not affected by acids, heat, or cold, and is widely used in kitchen pots and pans because it is nonstick and, therefore, easy to clean.
1939	*Nylon* was originally used for stockings but was soon discovered to be useful for many other things. Before nylon was invented, toothbrush bristles were made from animal hair!
1951	*Polyester* is most widely used in clothes, but also in bottles, film, and tape, and as a high-quality finish for guitars and pianos.
1953	*Lexan* is an extremely hard material—used in astronauts' helmets, windscreens, dashboards, computer laptop cases, CDs, DVDs, and cell phones.
1954	*Polystyrene* is used as a packing and building material.
1965	*Kevlar* is used to make bulletproof vest material for soldiers and police officers.
1979	*Fleece* is a warm and soft fabric-like material—used for blankets, jumpers, jackets, and other clothes.

PLASTIC POLLUTION IN THE OCEAN

The Great Pacific Garbage Patch is a huge area in the northern Pacific Ocean with high concentrations of plastic **debris**.

Charles Moore is a sailor and volunteer environmentalist who founded an organization called the Algalita Marine Research Foundation. In 1997, he was crossing the Pacific Ocean. He decided to take a shortcut across the edge of the North Pacific Ocean into the North Pacific Gyre. A **gyre** is a slowly moving clockwise spiral of currents created by a high-pressure system of air currents. It is like a very slow whirlpool that spins around but never drains. There, Moore saw an ocean he had never known. "There were shampoo caps and soap bottles and plastic bags and **fishing floats** as far as I could see," he said. "I was in the middle of the ocean, and there was nowhere I could go to avoid the plastic." Moore reported his findings to Curtis Ebbesmeyer, a scientist who studies oceans. Ebbesmeyer named the region the Eastern Garbage Patch. Later, media reports coined the name Great Pacific Garbage Patch.

Great Pacific
Garbage Patch

North Pacific Gyre

Pacific Ocean

■ The extent of the Great Pacific Garbage Patch has not been measured, but it ranges widely.

Charles Moore is credited with discovering the Great Pacific Garbage Patch. He has said that "the plastic soup we've made of the ocean is pretty universal, it's just a matter of degree."

How deep does it go?

Moore's discovery seemed to prove some scientists' suspicions about the existence of high litter concentrations in gyres. But Moore's claims have been controversial. In early reports, it sounded like the Patch was a huge floating mass of objects that could easily be spotted as a distinct mass. But the truth is different. The North Pacific Gyre has, like all the world's oceans, a lot of plastic pollution. However, from the surface, much of the ocean in the Patch area looks normal.

A closer look reveals a more disturbing picture. Scientists skimmed the ocean with fine nets and collected small particles called **nurdles** and **degraded** bits of plastic. Nurdles are plastic pellets that are the raw material for making plastic products. They are the most economical way to ship large amounts of solid plastic. Over 110 million tons of nurdles are shipped every year. The pellets come in container tanks, and at 22,000 to 33,000 nurdles per pound, there are about a billion of them in a shipping tanker. Unbelievable as it sounds, they are spilled all the time! This is because they often "escape" during the transfer, by vacuum hoses, from container tanks to factories, or they get washed away during storms from railroad lines at ports. Nurdles now represent about 10 percent of the litter tracked on beaches worldwide.

Nurdles and degraded plastic are dispersed over millions of square miles of ocean and extend deep in the water. It is, therefore, hard to say how big a patch actually is, or where a patch begins or ends. Some researchers have noted an Atlantic Ocean Patch and an Indian Ocean Patch.

Plastic soup

Scientists had previously thought plastics broke down only at very high temperatures and over hundreds of years. But in the ocean, plastics actually start decomposing fairly rapidly—within a year. It also happens at cooler temperatures than were first predicted: 86 degrees Fahrenheit (30 degrees Celsius).

Initially, this decomposition does not sound so worrying. After all, paper and wood decompose relatively harmlessly. But plastic in the ocean does not decompose harmlessly. Although decomposition is faster than first thought, it does not happen immediately, and it does not decompose completely. More worryingly, the breakdown is not a harmless process.

When plastic degrades, it **leaches** poisonous chemicals, called **toxins**, into the seas. The plastic soup found by researchers contains the toxic compounds polystyrene and bisphenol A (**BPA**). These compounds do not occur naturally in the ocean. They come from decomposing plastics. When polystyrene degrades, it breaks apart. The tiny parts of it sink because they are heavier than water.

Oceans, and the creatures that live in oceans, are at risk from an invisible threat of plastic-derived chemicals. However, toxins coming from plastic are not the only problem. Plastic also absorbs and gets coated with chemicals such as oil and other pollutants as they float in the sea. This makes the plastic sticky and harmful for wildlife that comes into contact with it. The toxins are concentrated in areas heavily littered with plastic garbage, such as in ocean gyres. As fish consume the plastic nurdles, these toxins enter our food chain, causing a health problem to people.

Oceans of plastic garbage

It is estimated that there are around 165 million tons of plastic in the oceans today.

Imagine a huge oil tanker sailing through the seas, gathering plastic garbage as it goes until it holds 275,000 tons of plastic. It would take 600 of these huge oil tankers to collect all of the plastic floating in our oceans. That's 17 percent of the world's fleet of oil tankers! They would also need fine nets to do the job.

This is what the soup of plastic samples collected in the North Pacific Gyre looks like.

It may be surprising to learn that only 20 percent of ocean plastic pollution comes from ocean-based sources, such as waste from ships and discarded fishing equipment. About 80 percent of marine debris comes from land-based sources. Waste from construction, ports, and factories, and garbage blown out of trash containers, trucks, and landfill sites, often makes its way into our oceans.

The most common source of plastic pollution (after nurdles and polystyrene pieces) comes from food containers and other forms of packaging. These items, together with plastic bags, represent the largest part of ocean debris.

More and more

Not only is there a lot of trash, but it is increasing at a rapid rate. Researchers speculate that plastic garbage increased five times in the Great Pacific Garbage Patch between 1997 and 2007. However, such increases are not limited only to ocean garbage patches that are far away from land. Near Japan's coast, the number of floating plastic particles increased by ten times in the ten years between the 1970s and 1980s, and then again ten times every two to three years in the 1990s. In the Antarctic Ocean, plastic debris increased 100 times during the early 1990s. These increases in plastic debris occurred at the same time that worldwide production of plastic fibers quadrupled. Given these statistics, it is likely that the problem of ocean garbage patches will get even worse before it gets better.

Around the world it goes

All oceans are interconnected, so floating garbage can travel around the world. In 1992, for example, 20 containers full of plastic toys were lost overboard from a Chinese ship going to Seattle, Washington. By 1994, some of the toys were appearing in Alaska. Others reached Iceland in 2000. Since then, there have been sightings of the toys in the Arctic, Pacific, and Atlantic Oceans.

TAKING IT PERSONALLY

The plastic litter that each person unintentionally dumps into the ocean in a year probably weighs more than you can lift!

CASE STUDY

Project Kaisei

One organization, Project Kaisei, is researching the Great Pacific Garbage Patch, educating people about it, and trying hard to clean it up. One of their initiatives involves testing better debris-gathering nets. Another important task is to "validate information on the scope and status of the Patch." In other words, they are collecting accurate information about the problem in order to inform and educate the public. They hope that, by monitoring the Patch, they can encourage people to help them in their efforts.

■ This ship in San Francisco Bay is the *Kaisei,* on its mission to inform the public about the Great Pacific Garbage Patch.

Damage and effect

In the ocean, plastic debris injures and kills ocean wildlife. In all, 267 marine species are affected by plastic refuse, including 86 percent of all sea turtle species, 44 percent of all seabird species, and 43 percent of all marine mammal species.

■ This fish was found trapped inside a floating polythene bag.

After swallowing plastic bags that have been thrown away, animals slowly starve to death because they cannot digest the plastic. Animals can also be killed as a result of plastic bag waste through suffocation, infection, drowning, and entanglement. In fact, plastic bags and other plastic debris can account for the deaths of one million birds, more than 100,000 whales, seals, and turtles, and countless fish worldwide every year.

About 44 percent of all seabirds eat plastic, sometimes with deadly consequences. Seabirds that feed on the ocean surface are more likely to consume plastic garbage that floats. One study found that about 98 percent of seabird chicks contained plastic and the quantity of plastic being eaten was increasing over time.

Beaked whales often swallow plastic bags by mistake because they strongly resemble their target prey, squid. Beluga and blue whales also suffer. Plastic bags often get caught in their **baleen**. The more they accidentally consume, the more at risk they are of choking, or having their intestines blocked by bags.

Turtles have also become victims of plastic waste. One in three loggerhead turtles, in the Adriatic Sea in Europe, has plastic in its intestine, according to researchers. The shallow waters of the Adriatic are important feeding grounds for the turtles as they develop into adults. However, the sea floor is one of the most polluted in Europe.

Green and hawksbill turtles in the Australian town of Moreton Bay, Queensland, have been dying due to plastic bag litter. Approximately 40 percent of the dead turtles studied there have plastics, including plastic bags, in their intestines. In the same way that the beaked whale mistakes plastic bags for squid, the turtles mistake floating plastic bags for jellyfish. In one case, a turtle only 18 inches (46 centimeters) long had over 50 plastic items in its stomach, including plastic bags, cling wrap, nylon rope, candy wrappers, and balloons.

Plastic in the food chain

One issue that may force people to reconsider the importance of plastic pollution is the effect it has on our own food chain. In 2008, researchers on a Pacific Gyre voyage began finding that fish are **ingesting** plastic fragments and debris. Of the 672 fish caught during that voyage, 35 percent had ingested plastic pieces. In the environment, toxins tend to accumulate in the food chain. The higher up the food chain toxins enter, the higher the concentration of toxins. We are just one step up on the food chain from when the toxins enter it: fish eat plastic; people eat fish.

The European Food Safety Authority (EFSA) reported on toxin levels found in food. After analyzing 7,000 samples of food and animal feed from 21 European countries, EFSA found the largest concentrations to be present in fish liver and fish oil. Overall, 8 percent of samples exceeded the maximum level of toxins permitted by **European Union legislation**.

So far, there are no firm conclusions about the effects of fish-ingested plastic on human health. In addition to BPA, there are toxins such as polychlorinated biphenyls and DDT that still linger in the environment from decades ago. Plastic absorbs these toxins, and the plastic is then eaten by fish in the ocean. Once absorbed, these pollutants can work their way up the food chain to humans. However, while it is true that some fish species are eating plastic, the number that do so is unknown. Also unknown is whether ingesting bits of polluted plastic is enough to transfer toxins from the plastic into the fish's fatty tissues where they can be consumed by humans.

PLASTIC POLLUTION ON LAND

Plastic pollution is pervasive on land, too. Farms work closely with nature, so many people would not normally associate them with plastic. However, there are many agricultural plastics to be found on the farm: dairy bags for holding milk, bags containing feed for animals, coverings for crops, wrappings for hay bales, and more. As in other areas of life, plastic has replaced many natural materials on the farm, such as concrete silos, glass greenhouses, and wire twine. Many of these substitutions make a lot of sense. Plastics are often safer to use and can improve production and efficiency. They also cost less and are easier to manage.

■ Bales of hay on farms are often wrapped in plastic.

The problem is that plastics are not always carefully disposed of on farms. About half of discarded farm plastic is burned because it is easier and less costly for farmers to dispose of it this way. But burning plastic has an environmental cost because it releases toxins such as BPA and other hazardous chemicals into the atmosphere. Waste plastic is also often plowed into the ground, where it can trap or injure wildlife.

One researcher trying to make a difference is Stephanie Barger. She is developing a program to collect and recycle the plastic film sheeting used to bale hay and hold dairy milk. She hopes that film sheeting and other farm plastics can be recycled into fence posts and refuse bags. Another exciting research possibility is converting agricultural waste plastic into fuel.

Landfills

Landfills are where most cities dispose of their refuse. They are garbage dumps in the land. Most landfills have a large proportion of plastic, with 93 percent of all plastic produced ending up in landfill. The volume is staggering. For example, people in the United States throw away 2.5 million plastic bottles every hour, which adds up to about 219 billion bottles a year. However, bottles are just the most visible plastic items. As we have learned on page 13, food containers and packaging make up the biggest amount of disposable waste.

Landfills introduce another problem. When rain falls over landfill sites, the water washes over the garbage and then seeps down into the ground. As the water drips through the landfill site, it absorbs chemicals from garbage and then leaks through the liners under landfill sites. This causes contamination to **groundwater** from BPA found in plastic refuse.

Plastic does decompose eventually, but it takes hundreds of years to do so on land. Decomposition is, therefore, not a sustainable method of waste disposal. Towns and countries are selling their land for refuse disposal, but since so much plastic is not biodegradable, the space available will eventually run out.

CASE STUDY

Bottled up bear

A bear cub in Florida was lucky to end up with nothing more than a sore head after getting it stuck in a plastic bottle for more than 10 days. The cub poked its head into the bottle and got stuck while digging through garbage looking for food with its mother. Animal welfare experts claimed that the cub was days away from death after not being able to eat or drink for more than a week. Luckily for the cub, biologists spotted it in time. They had to shoot the protective mother with a tranquilizer gun in order to safely catch the cub and remove the container from its head before its mother awoke. After making sure the cub was strong enough to return to the forest, the whole family of bears was moved to a less populated part of it.

■ A plastic jar can be a death trap for a young bear cub.

People vs. animals

In November 2008, in Australia, a 11½-foot (3.5-meter) long crocodile, which had been tagged as part of a government wildlife tracking program, was found dead. It had consumed 25 plastic shopping and garbage bags. This is a common fate for many wild animals.

Most people support the idea of protecting the environment and wildlife. However, for some people, the harm caused by plastic pollution is not enough to outweigh the benefits to human safety and convenience that plastic provides.

Many people do not believe that the effort and cost involved in protecting the environment is worth the inconvenience of limiting the use of plastic.

CAMELS DON'T NEED WATER BOTTLES

The desert and its inhabitants have also suffered from plastic pollution. Animals are eating the plastic left behind by visitors and tourists. They then choke on it or starve to death because the plastic blocks their intestines. Just like seabirds in the ocean, camels, sheep, goats, and cattle, as well as the protected Arabian oryx, sand gazelles, and other wildlife, are dying after ingesting plastic. From ocean to desert, there is no escape from plastic pollution.

Toxins in the home

BPA is found in many durable plastics, such as CDs, DVDs, electrical and electronic equipment, cars, sports safety equipment, food packaging, baby bottles, and food and drink containers. Therefore, people come into contact with BPA on a regular basis. It is difficult to avoid, and so the effects on human health are becoming a matter for concern.

BPA has been linked to increased instances of breast and prostate cancer and altered menstrual cycles. It has also been shown to cause diabetes in mice. BPA can leach out of plastic bottles and food containers and can, therefore, be ingested by people.

Some findings have shown that people can digest and pass BPA fairly easily. However, studies have not yet proved how harmful it is to human health to digest BPA in this way.

Softeners called phthalates are added to plastics to make them soft and flexible. Their presence in toys has been of primary concern, as children are much more vulnerable to toxic exposure. The European Union has banned the use of phthalates in children's toys.

Pick a number

The Resin Identification Code is an international standard for labeling plastics. It was developed to provide a consistent system for recycling. However, the code can also be used to recognize which are the safer plastics to have in the home and use for food packaging.

The numbers are shown within a "recycling triangle" on the packaging (for instance, on the bottom of a bottle). In the case of plastic food packaging, it is advisable to choose those labeled 2, 4, and 5. Packaging made with these plastics is not as big a threat to health as those with the other numbers. Bottles labeled with a 1 are safe for a single use and should not be refilled.

MICROWAVING FOOD IN PLASTIC CONTAINERS

Since the 1980s, plastic containers used for microwaving easy-to-prepare foods have become a common part of daily life. People use them to store leftovers. However, concern has developed over whether chemicals used in these plastic containers can leach out and pose a threat to health. Research is ongoing but, in the meantime, people can follow some simple guidelines to try to reduce risks.

- Do not microwave takeout containers, water bottles, or plastics for dairy or soft foods.

- Only use microwaveable takeout-food containers once.

- Do not microwave plastic bags.

- Ventilate containers by lifting the edge of the cover or lid.

- Do not allow plastic wrap to touch food during microwaving because it may melt onto it.

OTHER DANGERS

E-waste is discarded electronic items such as computers, TVs, cell phones, and DVD players. People in **developed countries** eventually get rid of their old electronic products and buy new ones. Plastic is used in all of these items, usually as casing. But what to do with discarded electronics, the disposal of e-waste, is becoming a huge problem.

High-tech refuse

In the United States, probably more than 70 percent of discarded computers, monitors, and TVs eventually end up in landfill sites. This is despite a growing number of laws that prohibit the dumping of e-waste because it may leak toxins such as lead, mercury, and arsenic into the ground. The rest may go to recycling centers, or get sent overseas as part of well-meaning assistance programs. However, sending electronic equipment overseas as part of assistance programs raises issues of its own.

Africa

When shipping containers of secondhand computers first began arriving in Ghana in the mid-2000s, the intention was to help close the digital divide with developed countries. But these donations from Western aid organizations and Ghanaian authorities had unexpected consequences. It is illegal to export scrap computers. However, dishonest exporters of old computers in the West learned to label scrap computers as "donations" and send them overseas.

Today, perhaps as many as 50 percent of computer shipments overseas are scrap. To dispose of the computers, people burn them in order to **salvage** the metals, such as copper, contained inside the plastic casing. This is sometimes called the new mining industry.

Burning the plastic computer cases releases harmful toxins into the air. The workers breathe in this toxic smoke directly—and often. Even more troubling is that most of these workers are only teenagers. They are children who must work because their families need the money to survive. The risks to health and physical growth from the toxins released by burning plastic are frightening.

CASE STUDY

Agbogbloshie

Imagine you had to spend every day of your life burning computers. This is a daily reality for thousands of children in countries such as Ghana and Nigeria. Outside of Ghana's largest city, in a slum next to the Korle Lagoon, one of the most polluted bodies of water on Earth, sits a smoldering wasteland.

A group of reporters is guided through the area by a 13-year-old boy named Alex. He takes them across a dead river to an area called Agbogbloshie. It has become one of the world's digital dumping grounds, where the West's e-waste piles up, hundreds of millions of tons of it each year. Alex works at the dump, as do many other boys.

The boys burn old foam on top of computers to melt away the plastic. They then collect the copper and iron from inside the computers to sell. They use magnets from old speakers to gather up the smaller pieces left behind at the burn site. They do this all day—and every day—at great risk to their health.

■ Terrible poverty contributes to the need to mine old computers.

■ The burning of plastic goes on in many countries.

Plastic air pollution

When any type of plastic is burned, it releases toxic chemicals into the air. According to the U.S. Department of Health, toxic chemicals released by burning e-waste can cause health problems such as cancer, leukemia, and asthma.

One of the poisons released through the burning of plastic is dioxin. It tends to stick to the waxy surface of leaves, where it can then enter the food chain. As you read on page 17, toxins that get into the food chain will eventually be consumed by people. Residue from burning also pollutes the soil and groundwater. It can enter the food chain through crops and livestock. In addition, certain chemicals released by burning can accumulate in animal fats. When people eat meat, fish, or dairy products, they then consume the chemicals.

This is not just a problem for **developing countries**. As we have seen on page 19, agricultural plastics are often burned near food sources. It is particularly important to reduce this health hazard to food production.

Watch where it goes!

Inspections in 2009 showed that 48 percent of waste exports from the European Union were illegal. And, in the United States, only about 10 percent of discarded computers are recycled again for use inside the United States. The United Nations estimates that 22 to 55 million tons of electronic waste are produced every year. There is clearly a need for laws to be more strongly **enforced** to ensure that the e-waste is disposed of responsibly. There should also be better monitoring of recycled computers, identifying where they are going and what condition they are in. Discarded computers sent overseas should actually work, to eliminate the temptation to "mine" them for metals.

WHAT DO YOU THINK?

Should developed countries ban sending computers to developing countries unless tougher rules are enforced? Can anything be done to protect the children and young people forced to work as salvagers? Could anything be done to make older computers worth more than the salvageable metals inside them?

Cooking circuit boards in China

Despite laws intended to stop it, hundreds of thousands of tons of e-waste from developed countries go to China. Recyclers avoid getting caught because there are enough Chinese businessmen eager to buy the waste right away and then sell it immediately.

The southern Chinese city of Guiyu is completely built around the e-waste trade. Miles and miles of nothing but old electronics stretch out as far as the eye can see. But there is literally a gold mine in those heaps of e-waste: tiny bits of gold found inside electronic circuit boards. Behind closed doors, women melt circuit boards to salvage computer chips for tiny amounts of gold. Every day it continues, with women breathing in toxic lead as they sit over the burners. Bit by bit, the gold is salvaged.

Circuit boards are unlikely to have even 0.0035 ounces (a tenth of a gram) of gold. Even if they did, it would take the circuit boards from ten computers to produce 0.035 ounces (1 gram) of gold, and 280 computers to get 1 ounce (28 grams) of gold. The average laptop weighs about 7¾ pounds (3.5 kilograms), and the average desktop computer at least 22 pounds (10 kilograms). This means that burning between between 2,160 and 6,170 pounds (980 and 2,800 kilograms) of computers is necessary to get just 1 ounce (28 grams) of gold. This is an enormous amount of heavy, laborious, and harmful work.

MINING HARD DRIVES FOR SECRETS

One lesser known problem is that criminals buy e-waste computer hard drives and then pay programmers to search them. Private financial data is sometimes found, such as credit card numbers and bank account information. The original owners may not have realized they left behind so much information. People have experienced identity theft and e-crimes as a result. It is not just individuals at risk. One hard drive obtained in Ghana contained contracts with U.S. military contractors, the U.S. defense intelligence agency, the space agency NASA, and even the Department of Homeland Security, the U.S. government agency that works to prevent terrorism.

In addition, environmental laws are not followed. A Hong Kong businessman said, "If you want to do it environmentally, you have to pay ... It isn't worth it to pay so much money." This goes against what Western environmentalists want to believe about e-waste recycling programs. Hong Kong ships millions of containers filled with goods to countries around the world. Profits can be made by loading the returning containers with cheap e-waste and then selling it off quickly. When these conditions were reported in the late 2000s, computer recycling organizations became concerned. They are working hard to make sure their computers are not going to be melted and mined, but sent instead to honest organizations.

India spins gold from garbage

India is another country with growing e-waste due to modernization and technology. But in contrast to China, India has some more positive stories to tell.

At a recycling plant in Bangalore, an Indian company is literally spinning the waste into gold. They refine the scrap in a safe environment and make watches and jewelry. They then market them as eco-friendly. Plants such as this one could become part of a global network of certified e-waste recyclers. The owner of another Indian recycling factory said, "In 2009, Indians bought more than seven million PCs. This generated 330,000 tons of electronic waste. They will come back to the waste stream sooner or later. It's a growing industry."

No day in the sun with plastic

It may not seem as significant as the damage to the environment and human health, but people also suffer when shorelines, bays, beaches, and rivers are overrun with floating plastic pollution. If plastic garbage accumulates in those areas, how can people swim or enjoy the shoreline? Seaside towns suffer economically because they must spend money to pay workers to dispose of the garbage. They may also lose out financially if tourists stop visiting their towns because of the pollution.

In one example, Jamaica spent around $294,000 to clean up Kingston Harbor in the wake of a tropical storm that caused plastic bottles to float and accumulate in large numbers. In towns where this happens frequently, daily garbage collection, or worse, piled-up bottles and plastics, mean trouble. Fewer tourists would come, damaging the local economy and disrupting people's lives.

In developing countries, if bays are choked with bottles and plastic refuse, the problem is not only a potential impact on tourism. The problem is the effect it has on local people's use of water for life and work. People cannot freely come and go from docks, or anchor their boats, when bays are clogged. For towns with fishing industries, the ability to fish is restricted.

There is more than one side to every issue. With plastic pollution, key points of disagreement are the amount of pollution that is dangerous, and how much effort should be expected of people to control or change their use of plastic.

Some people think that there is not enough plastic refuse to justify **enacting** laws to restrict or **regulate** plastics. They think there is not enough proof of harm. They say if it were truly hazardous, governments and society would regulate it.

But those who want more regulation say the problem is big enough to address. People who want more regulation and conservation say that the world cannot gamble with the environment's future.

◼ This river choked with plastic bottles is in Manila, in the Phillippines.

WHAT DO YOU THINK?

Does the convenience and low cost of plastics outweigh the effect it has on the environment?

ENFORCEMENT AND BANNING

People suggest that the laws against plastic pollution should be enforced. In the case of oceans, there are international laws. But enforcement is an issue when it comes to ocean plastic pollution.

It's the law!

The United Nations has laws called the Law of the Sea. Article 210 deals with pollution by dumping; Article 211, with pollution from vessels; and Article 216, with enforcement. Pollution of the ocean is basically not allowed. The law's key points are that plastic garbage cannot legally be disposed of in the oceans. This law applies whether the ocean is within 12 miles (19.3 kilometers) of a country, or whether citizens of a country are in the open ocean.

Another treaty is the International Convention for the Prevention of Pollution from Ships (known as MARPOL). Over 100 countries have agreed to this convention, including the 27 countries of the European Union.

■ The U.S. Coast Guard is ready to catch polluters.

The trouble with the Law of the Sea is that the United Nations does not have police boats to enforce laws. What's more, the ocean is so big that it would take many more boats than currently exist, simply to act as police boats. And much of the pollution does not come from ships at all!

Individual countries enact their own laws against plastic pollution, and for enforcement, too. The ocean law enforcement agency for the United States, the Coast Guard, has broad power to inspect boats for pollution violations. Even more specifically, the Congress passed laws in 1987 and in 2006 to prevent pollution by plastics and other refuse.

Fines are a punishment in, for example, Australia. Australia applies the MARPOL convention in Australian waters. Australian MARPOL regulations apply to Australian fishing boats wherever they are operating. Also, Australian laws can be applied against foreign fishing boats operating anywhere within Australia's 200-mile (320-kilometer) zone. Penalties may seem costly—up to A$260,000 (about $273,000) for individuals breaking the law, and A$1.3 million for companies. But a large multinational company dealing in hundreds of millions of dollars may consider A$1.3 million as just another cost of doing business. In such cases, it may be that citizens' groups can put pressure on companies to stop these activities by giving them embarrassing publicity.

Catching polluters at sea

How can polluters be caught? GPS devices may be a solution. Although not likely soon, it is possible that some day every boat could have a GPS. Boat owners suspected of causing pollution at sea could be monitored and caught if found to be in violation of environmental protection laws. This could also be a way for countries to monitor each other. Obviously, costs would be high to do this, especially for poorer countries. In any case, improvements are necessary in monitoring fishing boats and their activities, and enforcing fishing regulations. It might take more powerful satellites to monitor fishing boats effectively.

Enforcement raises many difficult questions. It might be difficult to enforce regulations in developing countries because of limited budgets. It is not realistic to expect the navies of developed countries to catch ocean litterbugs when their first duty is as a military protection force. No one knows how effective the Law of the Sea really is.

CASE STUDY

Fox River, Illinois

A plastics recycling company in the state of Illinois was caught dumping plastic chemicals in the Fox River in 2010. The story highlights how some companies claim to be concerned about the environment, but they really are not. It also shows how governments and people need to take action in order to look out for, and catch, environmental criminals.

South Elgin, Illinois police received a complaint from an area resident when he discovered foam and dead fish in the pond in his yard and in the nearby creek, which is located near the company. This led to a multi-agency investigation coordinated by the Office of the **Attorney General**.

■ Watchfulness is necessary to prevent river pollution like this.

Caught!

Arriving at the scene, a police officer saw a worker pouring liquid from a blue plastic drum into a storm drain at the facility. The drain flows to a creek, which empties downstream into the Fox River. Dead carp, catfish, frogs, and water snakes were pulled from the creek. Material taken from the storm drain was identified as an industrial cleaner that is toxic to fish and slow to biodegrade.

In June 2010, the chief executive officer of a wholesale plastics recycling business and one employee were arrested and charged for criminal water pollution. This is punishable by up to three years in prison and a $25,000 fine for each day of violation.

The operators of the facility dumped the chemicals simply because it saved money and time. Convenience and cost-savings are common priorities when the environment is in conflict with making money. But catching an environmental criminal, such as the recycling plant in Illinois, is a victory not just for the environment, but for people—for how they enjoy nature, and how they can work together to preserve that enjoyment for everyone.

Lots of cases

The Illinois case is not isolated. The U.S. Environmental Protection Agency (EPA) reported that 346 environmental crime cases were opened in 2010. This was an 11 percent decrease from 387 in 2009, but the second highest number of new cases since 2005. Of those, 289 criminal defendants were charged. Happily, there was an 88 percent conviction rate, resulting in $41 million in fines and compensation, $18 million of court-ordered environmental projects, and 72 years of prison.

The European Union steadily had environmental crimes numbering between 420 to 570 from the years 2003 to 2009. There were 31 environmental crimes in the United Kingdom in 2008 and 26 in 2009.

Spotlight on plastic bags

Plastic grocery store bags are among the most common shopping items on Earth. Their light weight, low cost, and water resistance make them very convenient for carrying things, from groceries to clothing. It is hard to imagine life without them. They weigh just a few grams and are so thin that they might seem harmless. But the sheer numbers are amazing.

Each year, across the world, some 500 billion plastic bags are used, ranging from large garbage bags to thick shopping totes to flimsy grocery bags. Only a tiny fraction of them are recycled, and most are just thrown away. That is when the problems start. The world is choking on carelessly discarded plastic bags.

Single-use plastic bags use up natural resources and energy. Plastic bags are made from nonrenewable polyethylene. When 1.1 tons of plastic bags is reused or recycled, the energy saved is equal to 11 barrels of oil. An estimated 3 million barrels of oil are required to produce 19 billion plastic bags. Only a few plastic grocery bags use recycled content, and most of those contain only around 5 percent recycled material.

Plastic bags last too long. They take between 20 and 1,000 years to break down. Even when they do, they do not biodegrade. They simply break apart into ever smaller pieces, eventually forming "plastic dust." The planet is being choked with bags. It is easy to imagine a single bag killing more than one animal over a very long lifetime on land and sea.

Paper or plastic?

To be fair, plastic bags have some good features. Producing plastic bags actually uses less energy and water than producing paper bags. It generates less air pollution and solid waste. Plastic bags also take up less space in a landfill.

But many of these bags never make it to landfills. Instead, they travel easily, floating—getting caught in fences, trees, and even in the throats of birds. They clog gutters, sewers, and waterways. So, when considering the "hidden costs" after bags are used, perhaps plastic bags are not so economical!

■ A blizzard of bags can spoil the scenery in the countryside.

Canvas tote bags

People are increasingly carrying plastic bags for reuse. But many people all over the world are starting to carry canvas or cloth bags. It is impossible to pinpoint exactly when this started. But an event in 2007 was a turning point. Designer Anya Hindmarch released the "I am Not a Plastic Bag" bag in collaboration with a global social-change group. It quickly became popular.

This may have been partly due to fashion. But people also switch for environmental reasons. Canvas bags are renewable and biodegradable and can last for years. Reusing them could reduce the number of plastic bags used and discarded every year. Also, even if it is for fashion, who cares? If it is good for the planet, then it is a "win–win" situation.

DID YOU KNOW?

The sight of plastic bags littering the landscape has become so common that the Irish have been known to call them their "national flag." South Africans have similarly dubbed them the "national flower."

Banning plastic bags

Plastic bags and bottles are choking the world. People have become more aware of that, and countries around the world have taken measures to limit or ban the use of throwaway plastic bags.

The first country do so was Bangladesh, which banned plastic bags in 2002. Following a severe typhoon, authorities discovered that millions of bags were clogging the country's flood drains, contributing to the damage. Because the drains were easily clogged by the bags, flooding was made that much worse!

Taxed

Also in 2002, Ireland took another approach and heavily taxed plastic bags. Use fell by 90 percent as a result, and the tax money that was gained paid for a greatly expanded recycling program. Plenty of other places have chosen not to ban plastic bags, but to discourage them through financial methods. In 2003, Taiwan started charging for plastic shopping bags, and restaurants were even required to charge for plastic utensils for takeout food. Plastic bags have been taxed since 2007 in Italy and Belgium. In Switzerland, Germany, and the Netherlands, the bags come with a fee.

■ This bag caught in a tree came from a nearby fast-food restaurant.

Larger economies have joined the cause. In 2003, Australia started a voluntary ban. Amazingly, consumption of the bags has dropped—90 percent of the country's retailers are cooperating. In 2007, the small town of Modbury became the first town to ban the plastic bag in the United Kingdom. There are efforts to make London plastic-bag-free by the time the Olympics come in 2012.

INVENTOR AND RECYCLER

In the 1970s, Gordon Dancy invented the cheap plastic grocery bag that is now causing so much controversy. At the time, plastic was considered the future, and Dancy thought that by emphasizing plastic he could help save trees. By the time he retired, however, he had come to believe that plastic bags were an environmental problem. In his retirement, he founded a company to promote their recycling.

In 2005, France placed a ban on all nonbiodegradable plastic bags that went into effect in 2010. Italy also banned the same kind of plastic bags in 2010, and China has already prohibited bags less than 0.025 millimeter thick. Rwanda banned plastic bags in 2006, while in Mexico, Mexico City adopted a ban in 2009. In India, cities and regions including Delhi, Mumbai, Karwar, Tirumala, Vasco, and RaJasthan all have a ban on the plastic bag.

In the United States, however, the plastics industry is powerful and argues that jobs will disappear if trade in plastic bags is reduced. Yet, even in the United States, the no-bags campaign is increasing. In 2008, New York State introduced a "reduce, reuse, and recycle" policy for grocery bags. In 2007, San Francisco banned plastic bags altogether. A similar ban exists in coastal North Carolina and was recently passed in Portland, Oregon. It looks like a trend is starting.

"Our country consumes a huge amount of plastic shopping bags ... [This has caused] a serious waste of energy and resources and environmental pollution because of excessive usage, inadequate recycling and other reasons."
An official on China's State Council

CASE STUDY

Concord, Massachusetts

Concord, Massachusetts passed an **ordinance** (city law) banning all bottled water (not just those in government use), in an effort to eliminate the bottles and the disposal problem they become. Concord thus became the first place in the United States to ban the sale of bottled water. The state Attorney General removed the ban because she was unsure if the ban violated rights of individuals and companies. But the town is planning to pass the ordinance once again.

The ordinance's passage was led by an 82-year-old woman, Jean Hill. "All these discarded bottles are damaging our planet and creating more pollution on our streets," she said. Even if the ban was not perfectly legal, she said that an important issue has been raised. However, the town clerk thought residents passed the ordinance without considering the practical issues. She said it was "more of a philosophical statement than actual legislation."

■ The pollution caused by plastic bottles has led ordinary citizens to campaign against their use.

CASE STUDY

Bundanoon, Australia

One town did not have to worry about narrow legal boundaries. Plastic bottles were removed from shelves in late September 2009 in the Australian town of Bundanoon. A ban on commercially bottled water—believed to be a world first—went into effect. The ban meant that bottled water was no longer sold in Bundanoon. Instead, reusable bottles went on sale, which can be refilled for free at new drinking fountains. Bundanoon residents cheered when the ban was passed by a nearly **unanimous** vote. Locals marched through the town the weekend the ban started. There was no legal problem with the ban because it was viewed as solely a local, town decision. It was, therefore, not an extensive violation of individual human rights.

Banning plastic bottles

Since the late 2000s, bottled water has become another target for banning, just like plastic bags. And some places have banned bottled water. But there are also problems in doing this.

One reason bans have started is economics. Companies that had bought bottled water for their employees began to return to tap water again because it is no threat to health—and it is cheaper. Environmental concerns also became a motivation. Whatever the reason, a 2010 survey of 101 U.S. cities, including San Francisco, Chicago, Seattle, and Phoenix, showed that 47 of them had some kind of ban on bottled water in city offices. Italy has banned not just the sale but even the carrying of plastic bottles along its Heritage Coastline. In the United Kingdom, Leeds University enacted a ban. Sometimes, however, the extent of a ban can introduce challenges.

RECYCLING

Plastics are a pollution problem, and societies all around the world realize that they need to think about how to dispose of them responsibly. Recycling might be even more effective in dealing with the problem.

Recycling and responsible disposal are the best measures for reducing and controlling e-waste. We also need improved supervision of e-waste donation programs. Legislation has made electronics recycling mandatory throughout the European Union, as it is in Japan and some other countries.

Recycling has problems, too

Recycling means reusing materials in order to make new things. Many materials can be recycled: paper, glass, metals such as aluminum and tin, and plastics. There are many different types of plastic, as we read on page 9. Therefore, the mix of chemicals in one type of plastic is very different from the mix in another. Unfortunately, these different chemical mixes mean that different types of plastic cannot be recycled all together or at once.

After plastic is collected for recycling, it goes to a solid waste recycling center. Next, it must be inspected and washed, and sorted into thermoplastic and thermoset (see page 7). Then they are processed into a raw material condition as much as possible, which, in the case of bottles, involves crushing them into bits. However, the purity of plastic tends to degrade with each recycling.

It is not practical to recycle many types of plastic at all, and sorting plastics can be both difficult and costly because of the chemicals they contain. Also, some materials take more time and money to process than others. Many communities and countries do not have the resources to process plastic themselves.

Recycling and down-cycling

Recycling plastics is not like recycling aluminum and glass. For example, a recycled glass bottle can be made economically into another one of similar quality. However, this is not the case with polyethylene (PET) bottles.

One outcome for plastics is that they get processed into other products such as doormats, textiles, carpets, or fiberfill for coats and sleeping bags. However, oil is used to produce these new products and, eventually, they will end up in a landfill site since they cannot be processed this way a third time. So, this is not recycling in the true sense of the word, as would be the case if they could be made into bottles again. Instead, PET bottles are **down-cycled**—changed into a material that is of lower quality than it was originally.

PET bottles are usually made with heavy metal catalysts that remain in the bottle's plastic to help with the breakdown when the plastic is heated for down-cycling. A catalyst is a substance that speeds up a chemical reaction while remaining unchanged itself. The problem is that the catalyst remains active even after the plastic is reprocessed. This weakens this second-generation plastic, making it impractical to process it again.

■ Recycling should become a habit from an early age.

WHAT DO YOU THINK?

It is good that PET bottles can be turned into something else. But how much does this process save resources and help to clean up pollution?

Don't people care?

Despite the difficulties, it is possible for plastics to be down-cycled or recycled. However, according to statistics, they are still more likely to be just thrown away. In the United States, only 7 percent of the total plastic waste generated in 2009 was recovered for recycling; 93 percent of plastics still ended up in landfill sites. In the United Kingdom, it is estimated that in 2010, about 25 percent of plastic waste was recycled.

What is the reason for such poor efforts? Recycling services are offered in most countries now, although the amount and activity varies from country to country, and even from city to city. Most recycling takes place in developed countries because they have more money and resources to do it. But there is a troubling fact associated with the process of recycling. The trucks used to collect recycling use fuel to transport it to the recycling centers, which in turn use fuel to run the processing machines. The recycling process itself can therefore be a factor in creating more pollution. People who are not ecologically motivated may feel that either way the environment will suffer, so why bother?

Biodegradable plastics

Plastics do eventually biodegrade, but as we have seen, this either comes about by becoming "plastic soup" in the ocean, or by taking about 1,000 years to do so on land. Many environmentalists hope that plastics that biodegrade more quickly may provide a solution. If plastic were more biodegradable, it would not harm the environment as much or at all. Some recently developed plastics biodegrade more quickly than before. They break down more rapidly because they are partly, or entirely, made from plant fibers. Not only are plants biodegradable, they are also a renewable resource.

One plant-based plastic that has been developed recently is made from corn. It could play an important role as a biodegradable replacement for petroleum-based plastic. But there is a serious issue with corn-based plastic. Only specially modified corn can be made into recyclable plastic; normal corn cannot. Also, the **composting** process required to break corn-based plastic down must be done at a special facility. It does not happen naturally as with other perishable refuse such as fruits and vegetables. With hope, scientists will find a solution to this problem soon. In the meantime, it is an obstacle standing in the way of an economical shift from oil-based to corn-based plastic.

Researchers working on biodegradable plastics still have many problems to resolve before these plastics can become an effective alternative to oil-based plastic. The scientific world is working on possible solutions.

■ This biodegradable plastic is made from a crop of corn!

FINDING SOLUTIONS

Despite the challenges addressed so far in reducing or eliminating plastics, scientists continue to create new options. The most promising are made of nanocarbons, products of recent nanotechnology. Nanotechnology is the branch of engineering that deals with manipulating material at a molecular (microscopic) level. Unlike polymer plastic, which comes from oil, nanocarbons are based on carbon, so they do not pollute as much.

Nanocarbons do all the things plastic can do. They are thin and made to stretch. They can be built into any shape. In addition, nanocarbon manufacturing is nonpolluting, unlike the production of plastic. Bowling balls, golf balls, sports equipment, and waterproof cotton balls already are being made of nanocarbons. It is exciting to think of other uses that could be found for them.

Three nanocarbons stand out: graphene, carbon nanotube, and carbon nanofoam. All three are 100 times stronger than steel; they are also lightweight and more resistant than Teflon. (Teflon is a material which resists things sticking to it. It is most commonly used in pots and pans.)

Greater use of nanocarbons would mean less oil would be used for disposable bottles, which would be helpful for oil conservation. The problem with nanocarbons is that they are not yet cheaper than plastic made from petroleum. However, if current rates of oil consumption continue, one day oil-based plastics will be more expensive to produce than carbon-based ones.

Does the planet have enough time to wait for that change? In the future, the whole world could be even more choked with plastic bottles than it is now! However, research is continuing in a number of areas. Scientists in India are working on composites called nanoclay, which are similar to plastic, but biodegrade more quickly.

CASE STUDY

Bag-eating bugs

In 2008, teenage junior scientist Daniel Burd developed a new way to decompose plastic bags. He conducted his experiment for a science fair project and ended up with a remarkable solution. Burd isolated bacteria that break down plastic and mixed a solution with them in a bucket with a plastic bag. His process decomposed the bag by 43 percent in just six weeks! There is hope that this could be done on a huge scale, but research is still ongoing about the viability of large factories with bag-eating bacteria. One pessimistic science website speculated that the bacteria could mutate and eat all the plastic in the world!

CASE STUDY

Mealworms eat polystyrene

Tseng I-Ching, a 16-year-old high school student from Taiwan, won a major prize at the 2009 Intel International Science and Engineering Fair for a project on polystyrene foam. The research project concerned a type of bacteria found in the digestive organs of mealworms. Tseng showed that these bacteria help the mealworms actually metabolize (digest) the polystyrene. Since polystyrene is not biodegradable, disposing of it has been a problem for scientists and environmentalists for some time. Tseng's groundbreaking project might be a possible solution.

CASE STUDY

Making oil from plastic

Another development was made by a company called Agilyx in the state of Oregon. Their process circulates hot air around cartridges filled with crushed plastic. This turns into gas which Agylix condenses into oil. They can convert about 11 tons of plastic each day into about 60 barrels of oil (about 2,400 gallons or 9,000 liters). Agilyx's customers are large plastic-waste producers (such as cities and industries) and recyclers. Agilyx's future will be interesting to see because they are an example of an emerging market, which means that they could explosively grow if customers consider it worthwhile to convert plastic to oil.

■ Reusable and recyclable cloth bags are a better option than single-use plastic bags.

Individual recycling and habit changing

To reduce plastic production and use, individuals must also consider changing their habits or routines. This is easier said than done, but possible measures could include the following:

- Plastic bottles – In addition to supporting the banning of plastic bottles, people could decrease their use. Many people already use glass bottles regularly, filling them with water, coffee, tea, or other drinks.

- Plastic containers – Glass jars can serve as alternatives to plastic food storage containers. Most milk bottles used to be glass but are now plastic, especially in the United States. In the United Kingdom, home delivery of glass bottles is not that uncommon and it is making a bit of a comeback. People like how milk in glass bottles is better for the environment—and it stays colder. They also like having it delivered to their door every morning. Perhaps these facts could encourage more people around the world to enjoy home delivery of milk in glass bottles.

- Cling wrap – Like plastic bags and bottles, cling wrap is wasteful because it is thrown away after a single use. Health issues are a concern, too. Some recent findings suggest that when it is used in microwave ovens, cling wrap may leach chemicals into food, particularly into foods with fat and oil. Natural cellophane works nearly as well as cling wrap. One kind comes from cottonwood trees. However, it costs more than petroleum-based cling wrap. Aluminum foil is another option, but aluminum is a finite resource. Overuse would raise the same recycling, conservation, and cost concerns.

More individual actions

Changing habits is part of the story. Sometimes recycling and reuse can be very interesting. One unique reuse of plastic was the *Plastiki*, a boat made entirely of 12,500 reclaimed plastic bottles. It sailed 8,000 miles (13,000 kilometers) across the Pacific Ocean to raise awareness about ocean plastic pollution. *Plastiki*'s skipper, David de Rothschild, read a United Nations environmental report about the world's oceans and wanted to prove that waste can be a reusable resource through design and construction. The *Plastiki* demonstrates the technical and creative possibilities in recycling.

Donating cell phones

Cell phones are cased in plastic. Donating your working cell phone and accessories is a positive, realistic option these days. When they are in good working order, organizations donate them to charities or sell them at a discount. This helps the environment, too, by saving energy and keeping plastic out of landfills. Also, precious metals are recovered without the horrifying labor conditions seen in China and Africa. Recycling saves these materials.

Cell phone collection programs are almost everywhere. Many organizations, such as cell phone companies, stores, network carriers, charities, and recycling sites have cell phone donation and recycling programs. Cell phones can even be mailed for recycling.

CASE STUDY

Wales

In the fall of 2010, volunteers on 40 beaches across Wales in the United Kingdom began a beach litter survey and clean-up operation. Organized by the Marine Conservation Society (MCS), by 2015 the group aims to reduce the litter on British beaches by half. The job will be big. On one beach, volunteers filled 25 garbage bags by clearing just 100 feet (300 meters) of beach. Across the United Kingdom, the litter on beaches has increased 146 percent since 1994.

There are two pieces of litter for every footstep on a beach.

"No one wants to visit a dirty beach. By cleaning Langland and other beaches around the Welsh coast, we'll be doing our bit for the environment, wildlife, and visitors alike."

Gill Bell, MCS Welsh Officer

CASE STUDY

Florida

Green Teens in Malibu, Florida was formed following an environmental workshop in 2008. Its goal is to preserve the environment, ocean, and marine life. They came up with reusable bags made from parachute material which they branded with a logo and **mottos**. They then took the bags and their concerns to a city council meeting, which followed their recommendations.

Club members feel that they are making the world a better place to live. In November 2010, a new ordinance went into effect in Malibu thanks to Green Teens. The ordinance bans the use of all kinds of nonreusable plastic bags throughout the city.

■ It takes volunteers a lot of garbage bags and a lot of time to clear up a beach, but it is worth the effort.

EDUCATION AND AWARENESS

With a topic as big as plastic pollution, it is hard to know what to think. The internet is the main source of information and learning these days. But with so much information, it is sometimes hard to sort it out confidently. Which facts are "best" and "most true"? Which facts should be emphasized in making decisions? Relying on scientific data is always important, but where is such information found, especially on the web?

Web tips

Websites that end with .org, .gov, and .edu are usually reliable. They are connected to, or operated by, educational institutions, the government, or other reputable organizations. Their purpose is not to make money. A site connected to plastic companies might understate risks. On the other hand, some organizations say all plastics should be eliminated at once, no matter that it is costly or removes helpful products. Those kinds of organizations probably are too extreme. So, when looking at individual sites, .com and .net sites are acceptable as starting points, but double-check facts elsewhere.

Without facts and true information, discussion and problem-solving cannot take place. People must also be careful, however, in how they use facts. Writers weave facts into their explanations to try and be persuasive. But even accurate facts can be used for conclusions and ideas that do not seem to fit the facts. You still must decide for yourself how reasonable an idea or an opinion is. Ask yourself as you read and research: do the details sound sensible and fair? Does the writer's position sound outrageous or especially angry?

Getting out there

Although the web is a good starting point, going to forums and meetings is helpful, too. Campaigns can be started online, in communities, or at schools. They can take the form of protests to confront people directly to force answers.

Media awareness and campaigns

Media reports about the Great Pacific Garbage Patch brought it to people's attention, which then kindled a lot of action. People must also work with the media for environmental causes, such as the campaign against the plastic factory in Illinois (see page 38). So, read, watch, and stay aware.

Organizations run campaigns but some—such as Algalita and Project Kaisei (see pages 10 and 15)—do a lot more. Algalita has a range of activities, from visiting the ocean to offering teaching material to having public information sessions to offering research. This kind of organization is ideal for learning and for spreading awareness. In the United Kingdom, the Plastics 2020 Challenge hosts a series of online debates on its website. The debates are framed around the Four Rs: Reduce, Reuse, Recycle, Recover. They also include discussions about the use, reuse, and disposal of plastics.

Getting personal: you and your elders

Numerous parents have reported that they never thought about the environment until their children made them think about it. They now consider the world they are leaving to the next generation.

This protester in Tirana, Albania was taking part in a demonstration against the government's plans to accept waste from other countries.

CASE STUDY

TED^x

TED stands for Technology, Entertainment, and Design. In the spirit of ideas worth spreading, TED^x is a program that brings people together to share ideas, with x indicating that it is a local, independently organized event. At a TED^x event, video and live speakers combine to spark deep discussion and connection in a small group. The TED Conference provides general guidance for the TED^x program.

TED^x Great Pacific Garbage Patch

TED^x Great Pacific Garbage Patch focused on the global plastic pollution problem. Two TED^x speakers were Charles Moore (see pages 10–11) and David de Rothschild, the creator and skipper of the *Plastiki* (see page 50). The event spurred more than 75 "watch parties" in places around the world where people gathered to listen to the speakers over the internet. A gathering of people with a purpose probably felt more energy and motivation than if they had watched alone or in a small group to discuss the TED^x events.

Challenging the world

TED^x Great Pacific Garbage Patch issued four challenges to the world:

1. To individuals and businesses: refuse disposable plastics

2. To manufacturers of plastic packaging and to manufacturers of plastic products:

- accept a voluntary cap on nonbiodegradable products, and begin investing resources into developing a new generation of plastic product—plant-based, nontoxic in any stage of its existence, and biodegradable.
- own the responsibility of your product until the very end. The packaging you choose for your products is your responsibility, not the buyer's.

- rethink the design of products—in order to reduce both the carbon footprint and plastic footprint of your goods shipped around the world.

3. To policy-makers and political leaders around the globe:

- adopt and support policies that support individuals and businesses in their efforts to eliminate disposable plastics.
- adopt policies that create economic incentives for businesses who reduce their plastic footprint.

4. To all nations threatened by plastic pollution: come together and form a union against the damage of plastic to your environment, economic well-being, and public health.

JD Russo

JD Russo is a member of the Plastic Pollution Coalition Advisory Council. He is student at Carmel High School in California and a strong supporter of alternatives to plastic. He believes in the power of the public to effect change and that people need to be personally connected to the issues. JD works at the Monterey Bay Aquarium as a volunteer guide. He also was a speaker on the web for TED[x] Great Pacific Garbage Patch, even though he was only a teenager at the time. JD's story shows how the web can empower anyone, no matter what age. It also shows the web's power in another way: how action for movements and causes has no boundaries.

"We must raise not just more awareness, but raise care."
JD Russo

ENVIRONMENT TIMELINE

1862	First synthetic plastic made by Alexander Parkesine
1869	Celluloid (first used for billiard balls, but by 1890s used more for photo film) is invented
1907	Bakelite (the first fully synthetic resin to become commercially successful) is invented
1908	Cellophane (not yet moisture-proof) is invented
1912	Landfills are introduced in England
1920	PVC (polyvinyl chloride) is invented
1925	Industry magazine *Plastics* comes out; the word *plastic* gains current meaning and usage
1927	Moisture-proof cellophane comes out. Huge sales follow in the next ten years.
1933	Polyethylene is invented
1938	Teflon is invented
1939	Nylon is invented
1948	ABS (often used for toys) is invented
1951	Polyester fabric (Dacron) is invented
1952	Deadly smog episodes in London draw attention to air quality
1953	Lexon (super-hard, used for helmets and electronics' casings) is invented
1954	Polystyrene foam (Styrofoam) is invented

1962	*Silent Spring*, a landmark book drawing attention to environmentalism, is published
1965	Kevlar (high strength, used in bulletproof vests) is invented
1969	Cuyahoga River in Cleveland burns due to oil and chemicals
1970	The Environmental Protection Agency is established in the U.S.A.
1971	Greenpeace, the international environmental protection group, is founded
1973	The Convention for the Prevention of Pollution from Ships (MARPOL) is adopted to restrict the release of pollution from ships
1974	Worldwatch Institute is formed, dedicated to researching environmental sustainability
1979	Fleece (warm and soft fabric) is invented
1980	Acid rain is identified by European scientists as culprit for half of harm to Black Forest
1984	In India, 20,000 people die following a deadly leak from a chemical pesticide plant
1985	Ozone hole is verified over the Antarctic by British scientists
1987	Montreal Protocols are signed, which pledge to fight ozone depletion
1992	Rio Earth Summit is held, creating a blueprint for planet sustainability

FACT FILE

Plastics 2020 Challenge

Here are some facts and figures that the Plastics 2020 Challenge has published on its website.

- A U.S. company has introduced a new plastic spray bottle that contains an interchangeable "pod" that can be reused for different cleaning products.

- The European plastics industry is worth more than $326 billion, providing employment for 1.6 million people.

- In 2011, 47 plastic associations from around the world agreed to the Global Declaration for Solutions on Marine Litter, committing to reducing little in the oceans.

- In 2007, 24 percent of plastic packaging in the United Kingdom was recycled.

- Italian fashion label Marin has launched a "Plastic Collection" including bags, T-shirts, and dresses made from recycled PVC plastic.

- The density of plastics thrown away into the United Kingdom ocean environment has increased by 146 percent since 1994.

- In December 2010, the United Nations Environmental Program (UNEP) published a report called "Waste and Climate Change" that includes a discussion of the importance of material recovery through recycling.

- It is thought that only 20 percent of litter in the ocean originates from sea-based activities such as fishing and sailing. The rest comes from poor waste management practices on the land and irresponsible littering by people.

- Ninety percent of litter floating in the oceans is plastic. Seventy percent of this will eventually sink.

- Plastics that might biodegrade over time on land will not do so in sea water, as the microorganisms that degrade plastics cannot survive in the ocean.

Marine Conservation Society

The Marine Conservation Society works to secure a future for the living seas and to save threatened sea life before it is lost forever. It has provided the following facts and figures.

- In 2010, Marine Conservation Society volunteers found 7,273 plastic bags in just one weekend.

- During the 2010 International Coastal Clean-up, which took place in over 100 countries worldwide, over 980,000 plastic bags were found.

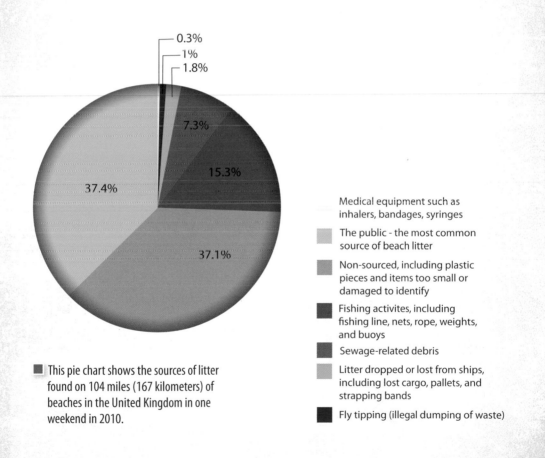

This pie chart shows the sources of litter found on 104 miles (167 kilometers) of beaches in the United Kingdom in one weekend in 2010.

Medical equipment such as inhalers, bandages, syringes

The public - the most common source of beach litter

Non-sourced, including plastic pieces and items too small or damaged to identify

Fishing activites, including fishing line, nets, rope, weights, and buoys

Sewage-related debris

Litter dropped or lost from ships, including lost cargo, pallets, and strapping bands

Fly tipping (illegal dumping of waste)

GLOSSARY

Attorney General top law enforcement lawyer in a state

baleen plates in a whale's mouth that filter food from the water

biodegrade break down

BPA bisphenol A, an industrial compound that is a component of several types of plastic

carbon substance from a group that includes coal, petroleum, asphalt, diamonds, and graphite

composting process of decomposing perishable refuse (fruits, vegetables) in order to turn it into fertilizer

debris remains of something that has been destroyed or broken up

degrade weaken and lose quality

developed country country in which the income is high enough to ensure that most people have a high level of well-being

developing country country in which the income is not yet high enough to ensure that most people have a high level of well-being

down-cycle convert waste materials or used products into new materials or products that are of lower quality and are less useful than the original materials

e-waste electronic items that are thrown away. These include computers, TVs, cell phones, and DVD players.

enact make into law

enforce ensure people follow a law or agreement, by physical or legal force

European Union organization of 27 European countries that decides on economic, social, and security policies that they have in common

fishing float plastic bobbers from which bait is suspended in water to lure and catch fish

groundwater water in the ground

gyre giant circular ocean surface current

ingest swallow, consume

landfill garbage placed in the ground, usually large amounts that become a land feature itself; sometimes called "dumps"

leach leak out from overflow or overabsorbtion in an item

legislation laws a society has; also, the passing of those laws by lawmakers

motto slogan or saying, usually associated with an individual or distinct group

nurdle small plastic pellet, usually about $\frac{1}{5}$ inch (5 millimeters) in diameter

ordinance city law

PET polyethylene terephthalate, the plastic used in disposable drink bottles

petroleum oily, flammable liquid that comes from below the ground and is processed into gasoline, plastics, and other products

polymer chain of a chemical unit such as carbon, hydrogen, oxygen, and/or silicon. Natural polymers are tar, shellac, tortoise shell, and horn.

polystyrene hard, clear plastic or foam that can be molded into objects

refine make free from impurities or unwanted material

regulate monitor or control something, usually through the law

salvage take something that has been thrown away and used for something else

thermoplastic one of the two categories of plastic. Thermoplastics can be melted and reused.

thermoset one of the two categories of plastic. Thermosets cannot be melted or reused; they can be ground up.

toxin poisonous substance that comes from living things

unanimous 100 percent agreement, with everyone voting the same way

FURTHER INFORMATION

Books

Coad, John. *Reducing Pollution* (Why Science Matters). Chicago: Heinemann-Raintree (2009).

Dorion, Christiane. *Pollution* (What If We Do Nothing?). Milwaukee, Wis.: Gareth Stevens (2009).

Snedden, Robert. *The Scientists Behind the Environment* (Sci-Hi). Chicago: Heinemann-Raintree (2011).

Websites

www.epa.gov/
The U.S. Environmental Protection Agency aims are to protect health and the environment.

plasticpollutioncoalition.org
As the name says, the Plastic Pollution Coalition specializes in information related to plastic pollution.

www.algalita.org
The Algalita Marine Research Foundation discovered and publicized the ocean garbage patches. They have much information and resources for all kinds of interested people (young students, reporters, academic researchers) about ocean pollution and marine life.

www.foe.co.uk/living/tips/tips.html
Go to the Friends of the Earth website for excellent tips, including how to get your computer and cell phone recycled.

www.ted.com/tedx

The TED^x "forum" or "event" website has TED events of all types. You might want to bookmark it simply to see what inspires people to organize a TED event. "Riveting talks by remarkable people, free to the world."

www.sas.org.uk/campaigns/marine-litter

Check out the Surfers Against Sewage website for information on their Return to Offender campaign and Motivocean Beach Clean program.

Topics for further research

- Recycling of plastic in poor countries
- Stories of arrests on ships polluting in the ocean
- Other substitute materials (such as canvas bags for plastic ones)
- Environmental laws in your county or town
- Interesting and unique reuse of plastic (for example, clothes made of plastic bags)
- The market for plastic antiques such as Bakelite
- Media images and references to plastic from the 1920s to the 1950s

INDEX